A Discovery Biography

David Glasgow Farragut

Our First Admiral

by Jean Lee Latham
illustrated by Paul Frame

CHELSEA JUNIORS
A division of Chelsea House Publishers
New York • Philadelphia

The Discovery Biographies have been prepared under the
educational supervision of Mary C. Austin, Ed.D.,
Reading Specialist and Professor of Education, Case
Western Reserve University.

Cover illustration: Bill Donahey

First Chelsea House edition 1991

1 3 5 7 9 8 6 4 2

ISBN   0-7910-1438-X

Contents

David G. Farragut:
Our First Admiral

CHAPTER

1 The Letter for Father . . 5

2 Captain Porter's Promise . . 11

3 Waiting 19

4 Midshipman Farragut . . 26

5 War! 33

6 Prize Master 41

7 Stranger in a Strange Land . 50

8 Which Flag? 56

9 "I Don't Intend To Fail!" . 61

10 Torpedoes! 67

11 First Admiral of the Navy . 75

Chapter *1*

The Letter for Father

Glasgow was not quite six when his brother William built a tree house in the big oak tree near their log cabin home in Tennessee.

The tree was so tall that William had to nail boards up the side of it to make a ladder to reach the first limbs.

"That's one place you won't tag after me!" he told Glasgow.

William was almost ten and tall for his age. He could grab the bottom board all right, but Glasgow could not reach it.

Glasgow didn't say anything. He just waited until the next morning when everybody was busy. Father was on the roof of their log cabin, fixing a hole. Mother was listening to William do his lessons.

"Now is the time," Glasgow thought. He dragged a small log over and leaned it against the tree. He crawled up to the bottom board. He began to climb.

Halfway up, he stopped and looked down. His stomach felt funny. "If I don't look down, I'll be all right," he told himself. "And when I'm in the navy, I'll climb lots higher than this!"

Father had been in the navy during the Revolutionary War. He had helped America beat the British. Now in 1807 the war had been over for a long time.

"I wish Father could be in the navy now," Glasgow thought. "Then I could go to sea with him."

Glasgow heard the sound of hoofbeats. Then a man's voice called, "Mr. Farragut. A letter for you, sir."

Glasgow forgot about the tree house. He heard Father calling Mother.

"Elizabeth. The navy! I'm going back in the navy!"

When Glasgow got back to the house, Father was walking up and down, waving the letter and smiling. "I'll be sailing master of a gunboat! We'll live in New Orleans! I'll go there in a week or two. But I don't want the rest of you to come until fall. Summer is yellow fever time. It's hard on newcomers."

"How will we go?" Mother asked.

"In a flatboat. I'll start to build it and have some men finish it. I'll get someone to bring you down the river."

"Can I be in the navy, too?" Glasgow asked.

William laughed at him. "Don't be silly. Little children can't join the navy."

"Don't call me little!" Glasgow ran at William, head down, fists doubled. He butted William in the stomach and began to pound him.

"Glasgow!" Father didn't sound stern very often, but he did now.

Glasgow stopped fighting. "Yes, sir?"

"I hope all my boys will be officers in the navy someday," Father said. "It would make me proud. But it's hard to get into the navy in peacetime."

"How could I do it?" Glasgow asked.

"First, you have to be a midshipman. Somebody important has to speak up for you, and say you would make a good officer. But nobody will speak up for a boy who can't hold his temper."

"Yes, sir," Glasgow said. "From now on," he thought, "I'll hold my temper."

"I'll get in the navy first," William said. "I'll be a midshipman when he is still just a child."

Glasgow doubled his fists and started at William again. Then he stopped. "What is New Orleans like?" he asked.

"A beautiful city!" Father said. "It's on the Mississippi River. The river is so deep that ships sail right up to the city. Dozens come there all the time."

"Ships!" Glasgow smiled. "I'll like that."

Chapter 2

Captain Porter's Promise

When the flatboat got to New Orleans, Glasgow stared with his mouth open at all the ships. He stared up and up at the tallest masts.

"Someday," he told himself, "I'll be in the navy. I'll climb the tallest mast on my ship, and be the lookout. I'll be the first to see an enemy ship. I'll warn the captain and save the ship."

Captain Porter, another navy man, came to the flatboat with Father. He was a nice old man with a big smile.

"So you like ships, do you?" he asked Glasgow. "Will you join the navy, too?"

"Father says it's hard to get into the navy in peacetime, sir."

"Don't worry, lad. As soon as you're old enough—eleven or twelve—I'll put in a good word for you."

"My goodness," Mother said. "Isn't that very young to join the navy?"

"No, ma'am. A boy who's going to be an officer has a lot to learn. You can't teach a duck to swim in the attic, and you can't train a navy man on dry land."

"But when do the boys go to school?"

"Oh, they go to school on the ship, ma'am. A navy ship of any size always has a chaplain—a preacher. He preaches and teaches both."

"He teaches book learning," Father explained. "The officers teach the boys all the important things."

"You'd be surprised how fast they learn, ma'am," the captain said. "An officer shouts an order. Then every midshipman on deck yells the order after him. That way, the 'middy' learns the orders and he sees what they mean."

"I'll get in the navy first," William said. "I'm older."

Glasgow clenched both his fists and counted to ten.

The next spring William did join the navy as a midshipman. He strutted home in his blue coat and shiny buttons.

Glasgow ran out of the house and sat by the water. Why did William always have to be older?

Captain Porter followed Glasgow to the water. "How would you like to go fishing with me?" he asked. Father and the captain each had rowboats.

For a while they both fished without talking. Then the captain said, "Your turn will come, lad. I promised you. When David Porter makes a promise, he keeps it. You believe me, don't you?"

"Yes, sir. You're my good friend."

But one day in June, Father ran into the house calling, "Elizabeth, get a bed ready!"

Two men carried Captain Porter in.

"Sunstroke," Father said. "He'd been fishing. I found him in his boat." He looked down at the cradle where the new baby, Elizabeth, slept, "I hate to bother you with a sick person, dear.

I know that you have your hands full."

"I'll help take care of the captain," Glasgow said. "He's my good friend."

"You can help, dear," Mother said. "Play outside with the little ones, so it will be quiet for the captain."

Three days later a neighbor called him to come to the house. She had the baby in her arms. "You're all coming over to my house, Glasgow. Bring the little ones."

"Where's Mother?"

"She doesn't feel good."

"Who's taking care of the captain?"

"Mrs. Willis is taking care of both of them. Come along, dear."

A week passed. One day Glasgow heard a woman say, "Poor Mr. Farragut. With all those children!"

What in the world did she mean? Father liked children.

At last the neighbor took Glasgow home.

Father was sitting in a chair, staring at the floor. He did not look up.

"I took good care of the little ones," Glasgow said.

Father did not answer.

"How's Captain Porter?"

Still Father didn't speak. The neighbor said, "The poor man's dead."

The house was very still.

Glasgow swallowed hard. "Where is Mother?"

Father bowed his head in his hands.

"She's gone, too, poor dear," the neighbor said sadly. "It was the yellow fever."

Chapter *3*

Waiting

For the next few months Glasgow was alone with his father. Neighbors took care of the little ones.

The days weren't so lonely. Glasgow went with Father on his gunboat. Its job was to sail up and down the rivers and inlets around New Orleans, on lookout for pirates or enemy ships.

Father was patient. He answered Glasgow's questions all day. But at night he only sat and stared. Many times Glasgow cried himself to sleep.

The next summer was even lonelier.

Father bought a farm 100 miles east of New Orleans, on a river that ran into the sea. He went back and forth to New Orleans in a little sailboat.

A man and his wife took care of the farm and the children. There were three of them at home. A neighbor was bringing up the baby, Elizabeth. George was four, Nancy was six, and Glasgow was eight.

Sometimes he went to New Orleans with Father. The rest of the time he stayed on the farm and wondered if he would ever get to be in the navy.

One day, when Father was home, a young man came to see them in a boat.

"You look like Captain Porter, sir," Glasgow said. "He was my good friend."

"He was my father."

"Are you a captain, too, sir?"

"No, I'm just a commander. Maybe I'll never get to be a captain. It's hard to get ahead in the navy in peacetime."

"Commander Porter is in charge of the U. S. Naval Station at New Orleans," Father said. "He's doing fine."

The young man smiled. "Mr. Farragut, my wife and I know how much you did for my father when he was sick."

"He was our friend," Father said.

"Thank you. We'd like to do something for you. We'd like to take one of your boys to raise. I'll see that he gets in the navy if he wants to."

"I'll go!" Glasgow said. "I want to be in the navy."

Three days later he was in New Orleans in Commander Porter's home.

Mrs. Porter was a pretty young woman with curly, brown hair and blue eyes. "It's going to be nice to have a boy around the house," she said. "How long have you gone to school?"

"My mother taught me until . . ." After a while he said, "Since she's gone I haven't had any lessons."

"You'll have lessons with me in the mornings," Mrs. Porter said.

"And in the afternoons," Commander Porter said, "you will go to my office with me."

"Don't you ever go on a ship, sir?"

Commander Porter smiled. "You'd like a ship better, would you? Well, we'll see what we can do about that."

"It's too bad you can't be on a ship all the time, sir," Glasgow said.

"A navy man goes where the navy sends him. Maybe next time I'll go to sea," Commander Porter said.

But the next spring he had his orders. They were to go to the navy office in Washington, D.C.

"I'm just as glad he isn't going to sea," Mrs. Porter said. She had a little baby now, named William.

"We will go on a ship all the way to Washington, won't we?" Glasgow asked.

She laughed. "Yes, Glasgow, you'll really be on a ship at sea."

Father, Nancy, and little George were at the wharf to say good-bye when the ship sailed. Nancy blinked back tears. There was a lump in Glasgow's throat. He wondered when he would ever see them again.

On shipboard, he forgot about being lonesome. The first lieutenant lifted his speaking trumpet and began to give orders.

Glasgow snapped to attention. He was not a midshipman yet, but he knew how they learned the orders. As the officer gave commands, Glasgow whispered each one after him.

Every day he asked questions. At last an officer told him, "You're a walking question mark."

"I'm going to be a midshipman, sir. I have to learn these things."

"How old are you?"

"I'll be nine this summer, sir."

"Then you'll have plenty of time before you're a midshipman."

"Yes, sir. I know, sir."

Chapter *4*

Midshipman Farragut

In December of 1810 a letter came for Glasgow. The Porters were living in Chester, Pennsylvania, in a big gray stone house. Glasgow was going to school—and waiting to be old enough to join the navy. Now he stared at the letter.

"I wonder what it is?"

Commander Porter chuckled. "Why don't you open it and find out?"

Glasgow opened it. Then he shouted. "A midshipman! I'm a midshipman! And I'm only going-on-ten!"

"Good for you!" the Commander said.

"I may have command of a ship before too long. I'll ask for you to be one of my midshipmen."

"How soon, sir? Next week?"

"No, no! Maybe in six months."

Glasgow sighed. Six months seemed a long time. "I guess things are slow in peacetime, sir," he said.

"If things keep on the way they are, we'll be at war," Commander Porter said. "The English keep stopping our ships and taking our sailors to serve in their navy."

"Then we ought to be on our ship, sir, getting ready to fight."

Commander Porter chuckled. "We'll both have to wait for orders, Glasgow. But here is a book that will help you get ready."

The book was *The Practical Navigator* by Nathaniel Bowditch. It explained "sea terms." Glasgow studied until he knew whole pages by heart.

In August of 1811 Glasgow got his orders. He would report to the frigate *Essex*. Commander Porter would be the captain of the ship.

Glasgow had never seen such a big ship. He had never seen so many sailors and officers in one place. And everybody was bigger than he was. The officers smiled when they looked at him. The sailors saluted and called him "Mr. Farragut." But he thought they were laughing inside when they said it.

Glasgow remembered what Father had said about holding his temper. He kept his tongue between his teeth and smiled.

At last the day came to sail. Captain Porter came on board. Mr. Downes, his first lieutenant, lifted his trumpet and gave the orders to sail.

Glasgow and other midshipmen on deck shouted each order after Mr. Downes.

Glasgow's voice hadn't changed yet. "I sound like a girl," he thought. But he kept on shouting the orders.

When the *Essex* was at sea, Mr. Downes said, "Mr. Farragut, you seem to know those orders."

"Thank you, sir."

"How old are you?"

"I'm ten, sir."

"I see. Well, Mr. Farragut, it won't surprise me if you're a captain before you're 20."

"Thank you, sir."

The next day Mr. Downes gave orders for drill with the big guns.

Glasgow didn't know those orders. "All I'll have to do," he thought, "is to stand by the officer in charge of a gun, and say what he says."

He found that was not so easy. Down on the gun deck, over three dozen guns were booming and officers were shouting. He stood in a daze, his ears ringing.

After the drill, an officer snapped, "Mr. Farragut! You did not repeat my orders!"

"I couldn't keep up with them, sir."

"Humph. How old are you?"

"I'm ten, sir."

"Humph. It won't surprise me if you're still a midshipman when you're 30!"

Chapter 5

War!

In June of 1812, America went to war with England. Glasgow was not quite eleven, but he was at home on the *Essex*. He could climb aloft like a monkey and take his place on the highest yard.

He knew every order for handling guns and sails. He knew the meaning of every drumbeat or shrill of the pipes.

He had learned to fight with his sword and with his fists too. He made up in speed what he lacked in size.

Captain Porter believed in having his men ready for anything.

The *Essex* sailed to watch for enemy ships. What would it be like, Glasgow wondered, to be in a battle? Would he be afraid?

Captain Porter seemed to know what he was thinking. "When battle comes, Glasgow, a man is too proud to be afraid."

"Yes, sir." He hoped the captain was right.

When battle came, he found the captain was right—and wrong. He was afraid. His heart hammered and his mouth was dry. But he was too proud to show it.

When the *Essex* captured an enemy ship, the captain called it a prize ship.

He sent an officer to take charge of it. He was the prize master. The crew that went with him were the prize crew. The prize master sailed the captured ship back to an American port to be sold. Part of the money would go to the government. The rest of it would go to Captain Porter and the crew of the *Essex*.

In ten weeks the *Essex* captured nine prize ships. Everybody cheered.

She returned to port for more supplies. Glasgow and Captain Porter went home to Chester for a few days.

The Porters had a baby girl now, named Elizabeth. Glasgow looked at her and thought of his baby sister. She would be about five years old now. When would he see her again?

Mrs. Porter was very pale when they left. She tried to smile at them, but she could not.

When they were at sea, Captain Porter talked to his men. "We are going where no American warship has ever been before. We'll join two other ships and sail into the Pacific. We will capture British whalers and merchant ships. We'll capture enough to make us all rich for life!"

The men cheered wildly.

But months later they looked grim. The *Essex* had not found the other ships she was supposed to meet. She was far south in the Atlantic. What would she do now?

Again Captain Porter talked to his men. The *Essex* would go on alone.

Again all the men cheered. Glasgow yelled as loudly as the others.

But that night he lay awake. What would they find in the Pacific? Just whalers and merchant ships? Or would there be British warships? He knew the British navy had 50 ships to their one. What would they find in the Pacific?

They found whaling ships from both England and America. They captured British ships. Prize masters and crews from the *Essex* set out to sail some of them home to American ports.

One day an officer said to Glasgow, "You know, we can't take many more prize ships."

"Why not, sir?" Glasgow asked.

"We'll run out of officers to serve as prize masters."

Captain Porter began sending the prize ships to Valparaiso to be sold. That was a port in Chile, a country that was friendly to the United States.

Still they captured ships. One day they took nine.

Captain Porter kept one trim little vessel with his ship. He renamed her *Essex, Jr.* and put Mr. Downes in charge.

One day they had four prize ships ready to go to Valparaiso. They captured a whaler, the *Barclay*. The captain was a huge, bearded man with a mean mouth.

"Who is your navigator?" Captain Porter asked.

Captain Randall doubled his huge fist and looked at it. "He was a trouble-maker," he growled. "I got rid of him."

"Then I'll leave you aboard to navigate your ship," Captain Porter said. "But my prize master will be in charge. Is that clear?"

Randall glared, then he growled, "Aye, aye, sir. Who's your prize master?"

"Mr. Farragut will be in command."

Chapter 6

Prize Master

A prize master! And he was barely twelve years old! Glasgow did not know how long he stood in a daze, staring at nothing.

Captain Porter hailed the *Essex, Jr.* She would sail for Valparaiso now. The *Barclay* would join her as soon as she had her prize master and prize crew aboard.

Glasgow went below to get a few things. It seemed to take him forever. He was all thumbs. When he got back to the top deck his prize crew was ready.

Some were strapping big fellows. He wondered what they were thinking. He went to the *Barclay* with his men and the sullen captain.

The *Essex* sailed north. Captain Randall smiled and watched her go.

The *Essex, Jr.* was already well to the south. Glasgow felt very much alone. He lifted his trumpet. "Get those sails filled! We're bound for Valparaiso!"

"I'll be hanged if we are!" Randall bellowed. "Touch one rope without my orders and I'll shoot you like a dog!" He felt for his pistols, then ran below.

The prize crew stared at Glasgow.

He took a deep breath. "Let's get under way!"

For a moment there was silence. Then one man shouted, "Aye, aye, sir!"

Glasgow yelled down to the captain's cabin, "Randall! If you come on deck with your pistols, that's mutiny! I'll have you thrown overboard!"

The crew roared, "Aye, aye, sir!"

Glasgow heaved a big sigh. He felt a knot untie in his stomach.

In Valparaiso, Mr. Downes arranged for the sale of the prize ships. Then he took the prize crews aboard the *Essex, Jr.* and sailed north to join Captain Porter.

The *Essex* and the *Essex, Jr.* were back in Valparaiso early in 1814. One day a ship brought a warning. Two British warships, the *Phoebe* and the *Cherub,* were hunting for Captain Porter.

Glasgow's heart hammered. This battle would not be like fighting a single warship or capturing a whaler.

Pipes shrilled and drums beat the signal, "Clear for action!"

Glasgow looked at the guns. He knew the row of guns along each side of the *Essex* were all carronades. They could do a lot of damage at close range, but they could not shoot very far. What if the British had broadsides of long-range guns?

The British ships sailed into the harbor, alongside the *Essex*. Glasgow clenched his fists. He knew the British felt safe here. No ships were supposed to fight in the harbor of a country not at war.

Captain Hillyar leaned against a gun on the *Phoebe* and lifted his hand in salute. How was Captain Porter? As the British captain talked, he was sizing up the guns on the *Essex*. Glasgow saw

whole broadsides of long-range guns on the *Phoebe*.

The British ships got supplies, then left the harbor. They stayed in sight, offshore, watching the *Essex*.

Days dragged by. Then a sudden gale roared down and hit the *Essex*. The cable holding one of her anchors snapped. The other anchor pulled loose. The *Essex* was drifting out to sea, where the British could attack her.

Captain Porter ordered all sails set. He was going to try to escape the British. But another gale, stronger than the first, hit the ship. The *Essex* heeled over, snapped back, and there was a loud crack. The main topmast was broken. The captain tried to reach the harbor again, but could not.

Now the British ships came toward her. The *Essex* had some long-range guns. But they were no match for whole broadsides of long-range guns.

Soon every sail on the *Essex* hung in rags. Her masts were broken, her guns wrecked.

When a gunner fell, Glasgow took the man's place. When that gun was wrecked, he ran to another one.

When a powder boy was killed, Glasgow grabbed the leather powder bucket and ran below for more powder.

The ship was ablaze near the powder room. Desperate men fought the blaze.

At last Captain Porter surrendered. For the first time the *Essex* flew a white flag. It would be the last time, too. She would never sail again.

Chapter 7

Stranger in a Strange Land

Glasgow's thirteenth birthday was the saddest time he had ever known. He was a prisoner of war, going home to be traded for a British prisoner.

The officers tried to cheer him up.

"Don't hang your head, lad. You were a credit to the navy."

"You were the youngest prize master that ever commanded a ship."

"And you fought like a lion!"

"Yes, sir, you'll get a promotion out of that last battle!"

Glasgow's spine tingled. He had been a midshipman before he was ten. Would he be a lieutenant before he was fifteen?

Ten years later, in 1824, he thought of that hope and smiled grimly. He was 24, and still a midshipman. He had been at sea most of the last ten years. He had helped guard merchant ships in the Mediterranean Sea. He had hunted pirates in the West Indies. Once, when he was only 18, he had been acting first lieutenant on a ship. But he was still just a midshipman.

On shore, he was a stranger in a strange land. Father and young George were both dead. Glasgow had seen William and Nancy only once. He had never seen Elizabeth since she was a baby.

The Porters always said their home was his home. But now they had several children of their own. The younger ones did not know him. He felt like a stranger there too.

The sea was his only home. Would he ever get ahead there? Or would he be a midshipman all his life?

Two years later, in 1826, he walked the deck of a ship homeward bound and felt he was walking on air. He was Lieutenant Farragut now, and married to a wonderful girl.

Susan had believed in him. She had married him when he was still just a midshipman. She was so gay and happy. She saw the fun in everything.

When Glasgow landed in Norfolk, a doctor met him at the wharf.

"Mr. Farragut, I must talk to you."

Glasgow grabbed the doctor's arm. "Is it Susan? Is she sick? She'll get well, won't she? She's got to get well! She can't die! She can't!"

"Sometimes she'll wish she could die," the doctor said. "It's arthritis."

"What caused it?"

"Nobody knows the cause or the cure. We just know people have more pain with it than anybody should have to stand."

"Someone, somewhere, must be able to do something!"

The doctor shook his head sadly.

The doctor was right. Nothing helped. When Glasgow was home, he spent every spare minute with Susan, trying to make her more comfortable.

She never gave up hope. She would say, "I feel ever so much better today."

But Glasgow often awoke in the night and heard her crying with pain.

In 1840, after sixteen years of pain, she died. Glasgow wrote to the navy department. He asked for sea duty. He wanted to get away from Norfolk.

It was more than two years before he was in Norfolk again. He had not wanted to come. But orders brought him there.

Someone called, "Welcome home!"

"It's not home to me," he thought. "No place is home."

Once again he was a stranger in a strange land.

Chapter *8*

Which Flag?

At a party one night he met Virginia
Loyall. She was a slim young woman
with smooth dark hair and thoughtful
eyes.

"Heaven help me," he said to himself,
"I have forgotten how to talk to girls."
But Virginia was easy to talk to.

Next time someone called, "Welcome
home!" Glasgow smiled and said, "Thank
you. It's good to be home."

Two years later he was happier than he had ever hoped to be. He and Virginia were married and had a son named Loyall.

Glasgow was Commander Farragut now. He was more than 40 when that promotion came. He remembered that in 1809, young Mr. Porter had been a commander before he was 30. Captain Porter had resigned from the navy, and was now a United States consul.

In 1854 orders sent Glasgow and his family to California. The United States now stretched from the Atlantic to the Pacific. The nation needed a navy yard in the west to take care of ships on the Pacific Coast. Glasgow was to build that navy yard on Mare Island in San Francisco Bay.

A letter came soon to Mare Island. Glasgow was now Captain Farragut. He smiled to himself. Once he had dreamed of being a captain before he was 20.

Ten-year-old Loyall grinned at him and saluted. "Next, you'll be an admiral!"

"No, son, we don't have admirals in our navy."

"We ought to, just for you."

After four happy years, Glasgow's work at Mare Island was done. Orders sent him back to Norfolk, Virginia.

"I'm glad," Virginia said. "This has been wonderful, but Norfolk is home."

"Yes," he said, "Norfolk is home."

He remembered those words the spring of 1861. Trouble had been growing between the North and the South. Now it looked as though there would be war.

In April the State of Virginia joined the South. Glasgow was heartsick.

"You'll be the first admiral in the South," an officer said to Glasgow.

"But I'm staying with the Union," Glasgow told him.

"Don't be a fool, Farragut! You'll have no chance to serve in the North. They won't trust Southern officers. Besides, you're almost 60, aren't you?"

"Over 50 years ago," Glasgow said, "I swore to defend my country against all enemies, abroad—and at home!"

Cold eyes glared at him. "You can't talk that way in Norfolk, Farragut!"

"Then I can get out of Norfolk!" He turned and walked away.

As he walked home, he thought hard. What was Virginia going to say?

Chapter *9*

"I Don't Intend To Fail!"

He told Virginia what had happened. Her state had joined the South. Then he said, "Dear, I took an oath to defend my country. I can't go back on that oath."

"And I made a promise when I married you. Where you go, we go, too!"

They left Norfolk that day. Glasgow found a home for them in Hastings, a town north of New York City. He wrote to the Navy Department, gave them his address, and said he was waiting for orders. Then he waited . . . and waited.

Weeks dragged slowly by. "Virginia, why don't they send for me?" he asked.

"Maybe they don't need very many officers."

He spread a map. "They need every ship and every officer they have. Look at this coastline, from Virginia to the tip of Florida, and around the Gulf Coast to Mexico. The South controls all of it. They hold Charleston, South Carolina, and New Orleans, and Mobile, on the Gulf Coast. Those are some of the most important ports in the country. We have to blockade that coastline. We have to station ships all along it, to stop trade with foreign countries."

"I don't understand," she said.

"England and France will side with the South. England will want cotton for her mills. She will trade guns and bullets for it."

He walked the floor. "Why don't they send for me?"

In December of 1861 the Secretary of the Navy, Mr. Welles, sent for Glasgow. The Union had a special task for him— a very dangerous one.

"I'm ready!" Glasgow said.

"You are to take New Orleans. It won't be easy. The channel up the Mississippi is narrow. Two forts guard it, Fort Saint Philip, and Fort Jackson.

We must destroy those forts, then take the city."

"We can run past the forts," Glasgow said, "and take the city. When the city falls, the forts will surrender. They can't get supplies. We'll need a small army to hold the forts and the city after they fall."

"Experts say wooden ships can't run past these forts," Mr. Welles said. "We plan to have mortars on gunboats batter the forts down first."

Glasgow had seen mortar guns in action. They hurled shells high in the air, so they would fall inside a wall and explode. "I don't think mortars will be able to destroy the forts," he said. "But if that's your plan, I'll do as you say."

On April 18, Glasgow waited in the

Mississippi River for the mortar fleet to destroy the forts. After six days of shelling, the forts still stood.

He talked to the captain of the *Hartford*, his flagship. Early tomorrow morning, he said, the fleet would steam past the forts and take New Orleans.

"But, sir, if we fail to take . . . ."

"I don't intend to fail!"

Chapter *10*

Torpedoes!

Before dawn seventeen Union ships started past the forts. Guns roared. A huge raft, with fire blazing twenty feet high, came toward the *Hartford*. The flagship tried to dodge the raft, but went aground and got stuck in the mud. The fire raft came against her. Soon the *Hartford* was ablaze. The Confederates cheered wildly.

But Glasgow's men were trained for duty. They put out the fire, and got the *Hartford* off the mudbank.

At last the Union ships all passed the forts. The Confederate gunboats in the river above were no match for the Union ships.

The defenses of New Orleans were no match for the Union fleet, either. That proud city, too, had depended on the forts to stop the North.

Glasgow wrote his report to Mr. Welles. He had run past the forts and had taken New Orleans. Then the forts had fallen, as he had said they would. Now, he said, he should attack Mobile Bay. Next to New Orleans, Mobile was the most important port on the Gulf Coast. The best way to blockade Mobile was to enter the bay and take the forts that protected it. Fort Morgan was the strongest one.

The North cheered his victory. For the first time Congress voted to have admirals in the U.S. Navy. Glasgow became Rear Admiral Farragut. But the government would not agree that he should attack Mobile next. It was not until 1864 that Glasgow got orders to attack the forts in Mobile Bay.

He knew it was going to be much harder to take the forts now. The South had had a long time to get ready. Fort Morgan had huge guns. Glasgow's ships would have to sail under those guns. Most of the channel had been blocked with torpedoes—shells that would explode if a ship bumped into them.

Also, he knew the South was building the *Tennessee*, a ship called an ironclad ram. The whole ship was plated with iron. She had a front end of heavy logs, covered with iron, so she could ram a wooden ship and sink her.

Glasgow knew he could not fight the *Tennessee* with his deep-draft wooden ships. The ram could go into shallow water where his ships could not follow. Her long-range guns could batter him when his guns could not reach her.

When the navy would send him ironclads, he said, he could take Mobile Bay. It was August of 1864 before he got the ships he needed for that fight. He knew he must win that battle! The war had been going badly for the North. Many Northern people were ready to give up.

He talked to his captains. "The four ironclads will lead the way in. Our fourteen wooden ships will be lashed together in pairs, with a gunboat on the port side, away from Fort Morgan. The *Hartford* and her gunboat will lead the wooden ships."

"Let the *Brooklyn* lead the wooden ships!" his captains begged. "She has heavier guns in her bow. We can't risk losing you at the start of the battle!"

At last he agreed. The *Brooklyn* would lead, the *Hartford* would follow. They would go in with the morning tide.

"Now, one more thing," he said. "Your ships must not stop! They must not turn back! Even if your engines were wrecked, the gunboat lashed to you could carry you through with the tide. You must not stop! If you did, you'd block the channel. The ships behind you would be helpless."

The next morning the ships started in. The battle raged. Soon smoke hung over the *Hartford*. Glasgow climbed up into the rigging where he could see.

The *Tecumseh,* one of his ironclads, was too far to the left! If she hit a torpedo . . . . There was a dull boom. Water spurted high. The *Tecumseh* sank.

Glasgow ordered a boat lowered to pick up any men who had escaped. Then he turned to watch the action. The *Brooklyn* had stopped and was backing!

He yelled down to his captain, "Take the lead! Go around the *Brooklyn!*"

His signalman called, "The *Brooklyn* says there are torpedoes ahead, sir."

"Damn the torpedoes! Go ahead! Full speed!"

Chapter *11*

First Admiral of the Navy

Straight over the field of torpedoes the *Hartford* led the way. "If I explode a dozen of them," Glasgow thought, "some of our ships will get through. A man cannot ask for a better end than to die for his country."

But no more torpedoes exploded. Soon the Union ships were anchoring in Mobile Bay, out of reach of the guns of Fort Morgan. The *Tennessee* had retreated to shallow water, under Fort Morgan's guns. The wooden ships could not follow.

"The battle isn't won," a captain said, "until we take the *Tennessee*."

"I'm going in after her, myself, on an ironclad," Glasgow told him. "I'll start tonight, after dark. If Fort Morgan guns are fired, they'll hit friend as well as foe."

A lookout shouted, "The *Tennessee* is coming out!"

And there she was—one ironclad against the whole Union fleet. The wooden ships tried to ram her, but only damaged their own hulls. Finally one of the Union ironclads got behind the *Tennessee* and blasted at her with its fifteen-inch shells. At last she surrendered.

Glasgow had never been so tired in his life. He wrote to Virginia, "When I get home, all I want to do is rest."

When Glasgow reached New York City in the *Hartford*, he had no chance to rest. Everyone wanted to entertain him. They asked him to settle in New York City. They gave him a present of $50,000 to buy a home.

He hardly had time to get settled in his new home. He became Vice Admiral Farragut. He had to go to Washington for more celebrations in his honor.

In April all the North celebrated. The war was won! Soon afterward the North was draped in black. Lincoln was dead.

Glasgow was one of the pallbearers at his funeral. Later, he and other leaders of the North went with President Andrew Johnson on a tour of Northern cities. They begged the people to forget bitterness and heal the wounds of war.

In 1866 the nation again honored the man who had served them so long. Glasgow became the first Admiral of the United States Navy.

The summer of 1867 the whole world honored him. He commanded the fleet on a tour of European countries. The President surprised him by letting Virginia go with him on his flagship. And Loyall, who had graduated from West Point, joined them in Europe.

"I said you'd be an admiral!" he told his father.

In 1870 New York City and the nation honored him one last time. They stood with bowed heads as his funeral procession passed. Sixty years before, a small boy had vowed to "protect and defend his country." He kept that vow.